"Michael A. Caparrelli, PhD (abd) is a prolific and prophetic writer who possesses the unique gift of communication and the ability to bring clarity to complexity. I can count on one hand preachers that possess Michael's literary and oratory skills, integrity and transparency. We, who know the man personally, recognize what an intellectual and prophetic maverick he truly is—a special gift is among us for sure."

*—Bishop Jeffery A. Williams, D.Min, MPA*

"Don't hesitate for one moment to welcome Michael A. Caparrelli, PhD (abd) to speak. You won't be disappointed. He is a man regenerated by the Spirit of God and wanting to convey the same to others is his passion. As a man of great character and quality, he is highly interested in people and his audiences walk away better than they arrived. Michael speaks with both humor and intellect having been highly gifted by God to serve the body of Christ in every kind of venue."

*—Pasco A. Manzo President/CEO Teen Challenge*
*New England & New Jersey*

# Pen Your Pain Into Parables

## A TOOL FOR RECOVERY
### *Workbook*

Michael A. Caparrelli, *PhD. abd*

Published by UNMUTED Publications

Visit: unmuted.app
Contact: unmuted777@gmail.com

Back Cover Photo: Rebecca Daniele
(Facebook: *Radiance by Rebecca Photography)*
Interior illustration: Simone Spruce at *simonespruce.com*
Book Design: wordsintheworks.com

*Pen Your Pain Into Parables—A Tool for Recovery*
is available online and should be read ahead of this workbook.

Please join our *Pain Into Parables Facebook Book Club*
at Facebook.com/mcaparrelli

# FOREWARD
*Gary Blackard President & CEO, Adult & Teen Challenge USA*

Narrative thinking is a lost art in the church. Jesus spoke to us in parables (narratives). He along with all of the authors of the books of the Bible expressed themselves with narrative thinking under the Divine anointing of the Holy Spirit. The ability to tell one's story can be life-changing at times. The late poet Maya Angelou once stated, "There is no greater agony than bearing an untold story inside you." In his book *Pen Your Pain Into Parables*, Michael A. Caparrelli shares his personal journey, giving insights into his pain, his joy and his learning along the road of life. Michael shares the narrative framework tool P.IC.T.UR.E. and tells how each one of us can use this tool in addressing painful memories and emotions in general.

In the second letter to the Corinthian church, the Apostle Paul writes the following (2 Corinthians 1:3-5 ESV): *Blessed be the God and Father of our Lord Jesus Christ, the Father of mercies and God of all comfort, who comforts us in all our affliction, so that we may be able to comfort those who are in any affliction, with the comfort with which we ourselves are comforted by God. For as we share abundantly in Christ's sufferings, so through Christ we share abundantly in comfort too.*

In these verses, Paul shares that as we are comforted through our pains or afflictions, we are to share that same comfort with others who are suffering as well, recognizing the comfort comes from the Creator Himself.

There is power in sharing your story with others. This book gives insights into how to frame your story for both personal and external impact and influence. As you let the Lord heal and comfort you through narrative tools, you will be better equipped to help others struggling as well. Galatians 6:2 says *Bear one another's burdens, and so fulfill the law of Christ.* In order to effectively help others in pain, you must receive the healing, strength and comfort from our Lord for your own pain. This book is filled with stories and tools to help you do that. My prayer for every reader is that our Savior Jesus Christ will envelop your life, transform your hearts and minds, and will show you the power of your life story and what God can do in a changed life.

# INTRODUCTION
## *Welcome Aboard*

You are not merely reading a workbook. Rather, you are embarking upon a voyage of redemption from a painful past into a promising future. Although you will only translate one painful moment into a parable on this voyage, you will be equipped with the skills to decode other traumatic situations into parables of wisdom, strength and love. Make no mistake about it, by the end of this voyage, your posture will transform from being a *victim* to a *victor.*

As you change the way you look at everything, everything you look at will change. Instead of your past being a tragedy, it will become a story of how the Savior rescued you from the flames, and used the heat to refine you. Expect to be transformed in how you process your past, perceive your present, and anticipate your future.

Let's be clear: This voyage is not a substitute for spiritual disciplines, therapy or necessary medical treatment. Instead, it is a supplemental tool to help you overcome the traumatic moments of your life. You will discover that the truths you acquire on this voyage will intersect with your prayer life, bible study, therapy sessions and church commitments. This is a voyage that runs its course through your life's entire landscape.

It is recommended that you not take this voyage alone, but travel with a companion or companions throughout these sessions. You may embark upon this journey with your partner, friend, relative, church family, or fellow peers. Whomever you journey with, seek relationships built upon trust, transparency and truthfulness.

By embarking upon this voyage, you are declaring:

### *I will confront my HISTORY!*

"I will no longer run from the pain of my past. Instead, I will square-off with those difficult moments with the power of God, the filter of His Word and the support of other people."

*Key Bible Verse:*

"Pick up your mat, and walk" (John 5:11).


### *I will pen my AGONY!*

"I will no longer harbor my pain. Instead, I will express that pain into parables; stories that elaborate on how I became smarter, stronger and sweeter from what I endured."

*Key Bible Verse:*

"Oh, that my words were recorded, that they were inscribed on a scroll, that they were inscribed with an iron tool on lead, or engraved in a rock" (Job 19:23-24).


### *I will share my TESTIMONY.*

"I will no longer be ashamed of my past. Instead, I will share that story with others to inspire them to make their own quantum leap from being a being a *victim* to a *victor.*"

*Key Bible Verse:*

"They triumphed over him (the devil) by the blood of the Lamb and by the word of their testimony"(Rev. 12:11).

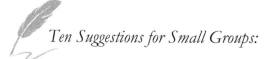

*Ten Suggestions for Small Groups:*

1. Participants should read the book *Pen Your Pain Into Parables* before the voyage begins.

2. Participants should meet in a comfortable, intimate location.

3. Begin every session with prayer for the help of the Holy Spirit.

4. Ground rules should be established, and recited at the opening of every meeting, that preserve order and protect the safety and anonymity of participants. Such ground rules as, but not limited to:

*—No interruptions or cross-talking when someone shares.*
*—Keep your sharing under five minutes.*
*—What's shared here, stays here.*
*—Share in the 'I' format, elaborating on your own experiences.*

5. Explore only one session in every meeting; a total of nine sessions.

6. Participants should complete homework each week; the return will only be as great as the investment.

7. Participants should be assigned roles. For instance, host the group, facilitate the discussion, set up the chairs, make the coffee, print any needed literature and remind participants with phone-calls, text messages, etc. By doing this, participants will acquire a sense of ownership.

8. Participants should be reminded to apply the three rules from the book in selecting what past experiences to write about. Those rules are listed as follows:

–The *Fish in Water* tip. Refrain from writing about any traumatic events you are still immersed in. You have to come out of something before you can understand what it's about. There's an Indian adage that says, "If you want a definition for water, don't ask a fish." A fish has no counter-perspective to understand what envelopes it; it's too immersed in its own situation to understand it.

–The *Boiling Pot* tip. Abstain from writing about any traumatic event that triggers psychological distress. You will need to see a therapist to talk these issues out before penning them out.

–The *Let Sleeping Dogs Lie* tip. Do not dig up issues that don't affect you in any way. If the dog is sleeping, let him sleep.

9. It is recommended that you join the Facebook Book Club known as "Pain Into Parables." On this page, you can share your thoughts, feelings and homework assignments with others on the same Journey.

10. Participants should refrain from playing therapist. This is not a therapy session, but a peer-facilitated support group grounded in the prescribed format of this book.

# P.I.C.T.U.R.E. Formula

Using the acronym, P.I.C.T.U.R.E., I offer you a tool that will help you pen your pain into parables. Truth be told, you could embark upon such a journey in multiple ways; however, this tool has proven to be helpful to me and others who have taken my classes. Each of these letters will be covered throughout the sessions of this voyage.

P – *Pain*

I – *Incident*

C – *Conflict*

T – *Truth*

U – *Unfolding Action*

R – *Resolution*

E – *Empathy*

# Session One: *Introduction*

1. Prayer for the help of the Holy Spirit.

2. Participants introduce themselves by saying: "My name is.........and one lesson I've learned in my life is........."

3. Participant reads the "Welcome Aboard" page.

4. Participant reads the "Ten Suggestions..." page.

5. The Facilitator, along with the consensus of the Participants, establishes ground rules and puts them on display within the setting.

6. The Facilitator assigns roles to the Participants.

7. The Facilitator provides information on whatever social media platform has been established, inviting the Participants to join that platform. The Facilitator elaborates upon the purpose of that social media platform is to share their home-work assignments related to that week's session.

8. Participants share two to three minutes on the part of the book that left the deepest impression upon their hearts.

9. Participants share a three to five minute synopsis (depending upon the size of the group) of their story.

10. The Facilitator closes the session in prayer.

# Homework Assignment One: *Introduction*

Elaborate on the reasons why you have embarked upon this journey. Also, share what you would like to accomplish over the next several months.

_____

_____

_____

_____

_____

_____

_____

_____

_____

_____

_____

_____

_____

_____

_____

_____

_____

_____

_____

_____

_____

_____

_____

_____

# Session Two: *P – Pain*

1. Prayer for the help of the Holy Spirit.

2. Read the ground rules.

3. Participants introduce themselves by saying: "My name is.........and one lesson I've learned in my life is........."

4. Participant reads the following bible verse about Motif Pain: "They have greatly oppressed me from my youth, but they have not gained the victory over me" (Ps.129:2).

5. Participant reads the following section from the book on Motif Pain: Begin the process by identifying a Motif Pain; a particular hurt that has stalked you all throughout your life. Perhaps it's the ache of rejection, abandonment, shame, inadequacy, failure, embarrassment or any other type of agony. Allow yourself the space to compose all of the related feelings, thoughts and even physical manifestations that occur as a result of this pain. Or, just write about an emotional pain bothering you in the present. More often than not, what bothers you now has stalked you from the days of your youth; perhaps a different set of circumstances but the same underlying emotions.

For instance, I have a friend of twenty years that regularly laments about being overlooked. One job after another, he shares with me the same feelings of being unnoticed or even snubbed by his supervisors and colleagues. That's his Motif Pain; a feeling that plagued him since he was a kid.

Trust where your pen guides you. If you start off writing about rejection, but it leads to shame, then go with it. The task of writing leads to self-discovery, shedding light upon various regions of our heart. The task of writing is very much like peeling back an onion; you begin with what's on the surface, and layer by layer, work towards the inner-core. It takes some time to get to what's getting at you. King Solomon says, "Counsel in the heart of man is like deep waters, but a man of understanding will draw it out" (Prov. 20:5).

One of the reasons why it takes time to reach the core of our pain is because we tend to avoid uncomfortable feelings. Also, some of us grew up in homes where we were made to feel guilty about what we feel. You should know that your feelings are not right or wrong; they just are. Pay no mind to those dismissive voices of your past. Instead, trust when your pen guides you to the core of your pain.

The real story is not what you went through, but what went through you. An explicit description of the people, places and things surrounding your pain will not result in the breakthrough you need. Freedom emerges when you discuss how these people, places and things affected you mentally, emotionally and spiritually. Be willing to look at what lies beneath the exterior. There, you will encounter the damage that's been done, and there you will experience the healing power of God.

6. Participants share on a Motif Pain from their own life in one to two sentences. Some examples are as follows:

*Rejection, Loneliness, Abandonment, Inadequacy, Jealousy, Fear, Regret, Shame, Grief/Loss, Anxiety, Obsession, Frustration, Mistrust, Resentment, Pessimism, Confusion, Paranoia, Hopelessness, Doubt, Emptiness, Insecurity, Guilt, Despair, Anger, Helpless, Worry, Sadness.*

7. Participants share examples about how their selected Motif Pain has affected their lives in less than three to five minutes.

8. The Facilitator reviews the homework assignment for this week. The Facilitator encourages the Participants to share their homework assignment on the social media platform throughout the week, relating to this session.

*What did the Holy Spirit show you in this session?*

_____

_____

_____

_____

_____

_____

_____

_____

_____

_____

_____

_____

_____

_____

_____

_____

_____

_____

_____

_____

_____

_____

_____

# Homework Assignment Two: *P – Pain*

"They have greatly oppressed me from my youth, but they have not gained the victory over me" (Ps.129:2).

1. What particular Motif Pain do you wish to explore, and why that pain?_____

_____

_____

_____

_____

_____

_____

_____

_____

_____

_____

_____

_____

2. How has this Motif Pain affected your life? Provide specific examples?_____

_____

_____

_____

_____

_____

_____

_____

_____

_____

_____

_____

3. Elaborate on the thoughts that accompany that Motif Pain.

_____

_____

_____

_____

_____

_____

_____

_____

_____

_____

_____

4. Elaborate on the circumstances that trigger this Motif Pain.

_____

_____

_____

_____

_____

_____

_____

_____

_____

_____

## Session Three: *I - Incident*

1. Prayer for the help of the Holy Spirit.

2. Read the ground rules.

3. Participants introduce themselves by saying: "My name is.........and one lesson I've learned in my life is........."

4. Participant reads the following bible verse about Incident: Jesus told his disciples, "In this world, you will have trouble. But take heart! I have overcome the world" (John 16:33).

5. Participant reads the following section from the book on your Incident: Think about your life as a movie with a sequence of scenes. Select a particular scene, or Incident, that corresponds with your Motif Pain. This Incident could have occurred anytime in your life prior to the present. The Incident does not have to be something catastrophic to be significant. A papercut can be just as painful to the flesh as being struck with a hammer. The Incident can be as minuscule as arriving late for gym class in the fifth grade; if the Incident pertains to your Motif Pain, then write about it. The only requirement for the selection of your Incident is that the situation be related to your Motif Pain.

For instance, let's assume your Motif Pain is shame. In that case, you might reflect upon showing up at your high school prom with a bulging, shiny pimple on your nose. You will explore the pain of shame within the context of your pimply prom. Resist the temptation to jump around to other scenes in your life; it is better to go deeper with one scene than go broader with a litany of scenes.

It is shocking how much one incident–such as the pimply prom–reveals to you about your pain.

When writing about the Incident, think it through with two different lenses. The first lens is called *Inspection,* in which you revisit the external details of that scene. Hark back to the car you drove, the songs played at the prom, the boy or girl you danced with, your hairstyle, your apparel, etc. Scientific research on memory shows that a person vividly dredges up the external elements associated with the pain they felt while discarding other details. For instance, one study revealed that a victim explicitly remembered the knife used in the attack while she forgot the clothing or vehicle of the attacker. In the pimply prom incident, you might recall a song lyric played at the venue that summarized your feelings while sitting next to your pretty date (e.g. *Beauty and the Beast*) or maybe the tomatoes on your salad that reminded you of the bulge on your nose. No pressure to remember everything; you are not a journalist who reports all of the facts. Instead, pay attention to those details that left an impression on your heart. Your memory itself is showing you what matters the most.

The second lens is called *Introspection,* in which you recall the feelings and thoughts that passed through you during that incident. Summon to mind the dread you felt when looking at your pimple in the mirror, the anxiety you experienced when your date arrived, the paranoia of all eyes being on you when you entered the school, etc. When you find your story, you remember what you went through (*Inspection*) as well as what went through you (*Introspection*).

6. Participants share about an Incident from their own life for two to three minutes, elaborating upon how it relates to their Motif Pain.

7. Participants share about their incident with *inspective* and *introspective* details for two to three minutes.

8. The Facilitator reviews the homework assignment for this week. The

Facilitator encourages the Participants to share their homework assignments on the social media platform throughout the week, relating to this session.

*What did the Holy Spirit show you in this session?*

_____

_____

_____

_____

_____

_____

_____

_____

_____

_____

_____

_____

_____

_____

_____

_____

_____

_____

_____

_____

_____

_____

_____

_____

# Homework Assignment Three: *I – Incident*

Jesus told his disciples, "In this world, you will have trouble. But take heart! I have overcome the world" (John 16:33).

1. What particular Incident do you wish to explore, and why that Incident?_____

_____

_____

_____

_____

_____

_____

_____

_____

_____

_____

2. Elaborate on the *Inspective* details of that Incident.

_____

_____

_____

_____

_____

_____

_____

_____

_____

_____

_____

_____

3. Elaborate on the *Introspective* details on that Incident.

_____

_____

_____

_____

_____

_____

_____

_____

_____

_____

_____

4. Elaborate on how this Incident relates to your Motif Pain.

_____

_____

_____

_____

_____

_____

_____

_____

_____

_____

# *Session Four: C – Conflict*

1. Prayer for the help of the Holy Spirit.

2. Read the ground rules.

3. Participants introduce themselves by saying: "My name is………and one lesson I've learned in my life is………"

4. Participant reads the following bible verse about the Conflict: "For our struggle is not against flesh and blood, but against the rulers, against the authorities, against the powers of this dark world and against the spiritual forces of evil in the heavenly realms" (Eph. 6:12).

5. Participant reads the following section from the book on your Conflict: The Conflict is the struggle you engage in within your story. Take some time to identify the conflict within the Incident you selected. On the surface, the Conflict might involve you and another person. Or, it might be between you and some system. In the case of the pimple, the Conflict involves you against your own adolescent biology. Without Conflict, your story is flat; it is the heartbeat of the story that gives it life and keeps it moving. As much as you complain about Conflict, if you had no struggles in your life, you would die slowly from agonizing monotony.

Below the surface, the Conflict is always YOU against YOU; a war with your own self-concept, ideas, feelings, fears, etc. Below the surface, it is an internal war with some underlying issue. The Apostle Paul sheds light on the real conflict we face in Ephesians 6:12 (NIV) when he says, For our struggle is not against flesh and blood, but against the rulers, against the authorities, against the powers of this dark world and against the spiritual forces of evil in the heavenly realms. Paul defines the essence of all Conflict—a spiritual combat with powers of darkness that plays out within the arena of our minds.

For instance, in the movie *Rocky*, the Conflict on the surface entails Rocky versus Apollo Creed. Below the surface, the Conflict involves Rocky versus his own inadequacy. The feud that Rocky wages with Apollo Creed merely provokes the real battle Rocky faces with his own inner demons. The real battle occurs not in the arena of your living room, workplace or church, but within the battlefield of your mind.

The most essential thing to know about Conflict is that it is the friction God utilizes to shape you. In Proverbs 27:17, King Solomon likens your Conflicts to "iron sharpening iron." The metaphor accentuates how friction with someone or something sharpens you, just as one piece of iron hones another piece of iron. The end-result of such strife is a refined object. All of that arguing you did with your siblings made you smarter. All of those fights you engaged in with your classmates made you stronger. When you think about your Conflicts, take into account the ways in which that Conflict honed your intellect, character and personality.

6. Participants share about the on-the-surface Conflict of their Incident for two to three minutes.

7. Participants share about the underlying Conflict of their Incident for three to five minutes.

8. The Facilitator reviews the homework assignment for this week. The Facilitator encourages the Participants to share their homework assignments on the social media platform throughout the week, relating to this session.

*What did the Holy Spirit show you in this session?*

# Homework Assignment Four: *C – Conflict*

"For our struggle is not against flesh and blood, but against the rulers, against the authorities, against the powers of this dark world and against the spiritual forces of evil in the heavenly realms" (Eph. 6:12).

1. Elaborate upon the on-the-surface Conflict of your incident.

_____

_____

_____

_____

_____

_____

_____

_____

_____

_____

_____

_____

_____

2. Elaborate upon the underlying Conflict of your Incident.

_____

_____

_____

_____

_____

_____

_____

_____

_____

_____

_____

_____

_____

3. Take into account all of the ways that your Conflicts honed you.

_____

_____

_____

_____

_____

_____

_____

_____

_____

_____

_____

_____

_____

_____

_____

_____

_____

_____

_____

_____

 Session Five:- *T – Truth*

1. Prayer for the help of the Holy Spirit.

2. Read the ground rules.

3. Participants introduce themselves by saying: "My name is.........and one lesson I've learned in my life is........."

4. Participant reads the following bible verse about Truth: "Then, you will know the truth and the truth will set you free" (John 8:32).

5. Participant reads the following section from the book on Truth: Now, we come to the touchstone of every parable. Now, we arrive at what distinguishes the parable from other short stories. What constitutes a parable is that it's entire composition hinges on a particular Truth. It's your job to unearth the precious Truth buried within the muck of the incident. When you undertake such a job, it is a prayerful, thoughtful and soul-searching experience but so worthwhile. When you unearth the Truth, it sets you free from particular toxic lies planted within your mind. Below is a catalogue of four different Truths that your incident may have taught you.

*A lesson to learn.* A teaching you learned, usually through the school of hard-knocks, about life. Something you figured out, typically through feeling the heat rather than seeing the light, about living in this world. For instance, in the parable of the feast in Luke 14, Jesus teaches us that you will be humiliated when you exalt yourself.

*A principle to practice.* A practical guideline you apply in order to reap the benefits it promises. For instance, in the parable of the unjust judge in Luke 18, Jesus teaches us about the principle of persistent prayer and how it pays off.

*A characteristic to emulate.* An honorable trait that someone exhibits and becomes a virtue to aspire after. An admirable attribute that reflects the character of God. For instance, in the parable of the Prodigal Son in Luke 15, Jesus illustrates the merciful love of God that does not treat someone according to their sins.

*An observation to remember.* Data acquired about human or divine nature that tempers your future expectations. For instance, in the parable of the two sons in Matthew 21, Jesus teaches us that a person should not be trusted based on their talk but only on how they walk. Once you dig up the truth from your past experience, state that truth in a brief, catchy manner; no more than two sentences. Avoid using cliché statements like "The early bird catches the worm" or "Let go and let God." Try your best to convey that truth in a fresh, original manner. Also, it is effective to wrap up the parable with stating that truth in the last sentence.

6. Participants share about a Truth they learned from their own life for two to three minutes, as well as how they learned it.

7. Participants share about how that Truth either serves as a lesson to learn, a principle to practice, an observation to remember or a characteristic to emulate.

8. Facilitator reviews the homework assignment for this week. Facilitator encourages the Participants to share their homework assignments on the social media platform throughout the week, relating to this session.

*What did the Holy Spirit show you in this session?*

_____
_____
_____
_____
_____
_____
_____
_____
_____
_____
_____
_____
_____
_____
_____
_____
_____
_____
_____
_____
_____
_____
_____
_____
_____
_____
_____

## *Homework Assignment Five: T—Truth*

"Then, you will know the truth and the truth will set you free" (John 8:32).

1. Elaborate upon a Truth you learned from your past, and how you learned it._____

_____

_____

_____

_____

_____

_____

_____

_____

_____

_____

_____

_____

_____

_____

2. Elaborate upon what kind of Truth it is—lesson, principle, observation, characteristic._____

_____

_____

_____

_____

_____

_____

_____

_____

_____

_____

_____

_____

_____

_____

3. Have you had any new opportunities in recent days to apply that Truth? Elaborate on those opportunities.

_____

_____

_____

_____

_____

_____

_____

_____

_____

_____

_____

_____

_____

_____

_____

_____

_____

_____

_____

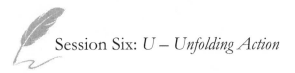

# Session Six: U – *Unfolding Action*

1. Prayer for the help of the Holy Spirit.

2. Read the ground rules.

3. Participants introduce themselves by saying: "My name is.........and one lesson I've learned in my life is........."

4. Participant reads the following bible verse about Unfolding Action: "After he had spent everything, there was a severe famine in that whole country, and he began to be in need...When he came to his senses, he said, 'How many of my father's hired servants have food to spare, and here I am starving to death! I will set out and go back to my father'" (Luke 15:14,17).

5. Participant reads the following section from the book on Unfolding Action: The Unfolding Action refers to the development of the story's tension from the beginning to the end of the incident. The Unfolding Action consists of three things, all of which are described below.

*Inciting Moment.* This is the small or big event in the beginning of the story that sets off the conflict. For instance, in the story about the pimply prom, the inciting moment could be the instant you noticed the glossy, colossal pimple on your nose while staring into your bathroom mirror.

*Rising Action.* This refers to the sequence of personal decisions and external happenings that increases the tension of the story. In the pimply prom story, the rising action could be all of your decisions to cure or hide the pimple which only make it worse.

*Climax.* This refers to the most intense part of the story, and it's turning point. In the pimply prom story, the climax could be the moment you kiss your date, allowing him/her a close-up view of your pimple.

6. Participants share about the Unfolding Action within their selected Incident: the Inciting Moment, the Rising Action and the Climax for three to six minutes

7. The Facilitator reviews the homework assignment for this week. The Facilitator encourages the Participants to share their homework assignment on the social media platform throughout the week, relating to this session.

*What did the Holy Spirit show you in this session?*

# Homework Assignment Six: *U – Unfolding Action*

"After he had spent everything, there was a severe famine in that whole country, and he began to be in need. When he came to his senses, he said, 'How many of my father's hired servants have food to spare, and here I am starving to death! I will set out and go back to my father'" (Luke 15:14,17).

Elaborate upon the Unfolding Action within the selected incident:
1. The Inciting Moment:

_____

_____

_____

_____

_____

_____

_____

_____

_____

_____

_____

_____

_____

_____

_____

_____

_____

_____

_____

_____

_____

_____

_____

_____

_____

_____

_____

2. The Rising Action:

_____

_____

_____

_____

_____

_____

_____

_____

_____

_____

_____

_____

_____

_____

_____

_____

_____

_____

_____

_____

_____

_____

_____

_____

_____

_____

3. The Climax:

_____

_____

_____

_____

_____

_____

_____

_____

_____

_____

_____

_____

_____

_____

_____

_____

_____

_____

_____

_____

_____

_____

_____

_____

_____

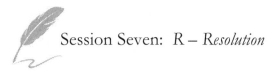

# Session Seven:  R – *Resolution*

1. Prayer for the help of the Holy Spirit.

2. Read the ground rules.

3. Participants introduce themselves by saying: "My name is.........and one lesson I've learned in my life is........."

4. Participant reads the following bible verse about Resolution: "Now, we who have believed enter that rest" (Heb. 4:3).

5. Participant reads the following section from the book on Resolution: In recovery from traumatic events, closure is something we seek. Closure is defined as 'a sense of acceptance that enables us to let go of what was in order to embrace what is.' Perhaps closure means an apology with an explanation from someone who wounded you. Maybe closure implies retribution or justice of some form for crimes committed against you. Perhaps closure involves the opportunity to vocalize your feelings to someone who injured you. But what happens when your offender will not apologize? What happens when your perpetrator moves to an undisclosed location, dies or refuses to grant you the opportunity to share what you feel? What happens when the jury finds your abuser, *Not Guilty?* The problem with seeking these kinds of closures is that you're placing your destiny in the hands of another person; in many cases, a person who has already proven to be heartless. Fortunately, true closure does not lie in someone's hands but dwells inside of your heart.
Haven't you noticed that the author has the final say-so in every story? Even the most powerful characters cannot usurp the power of the

author's pen. You are the author of your story (under the inspiration of God, of course). The people in your life are merely the characters. You decide how the story will end. You determine if your tale will culminate in tragedy or victory. In many stories, the antagonist refuses to change. In many stories, the antagonist continues to wreak havoc in the lives of people. Fortunately, it is not a change in the antagonist's behavior that guarantees a resolution. It is the pen of the author that offers a fulfilling resolution that alleviates inner turmoil.

The Resolution refers to the moment(s) that occurs after the climax, brings the story's tension to a close and leads to the final disclosure of truth. In the pimply prom story, the Resolution might entail your date complimenting you for your kindness—a moment that alleviates tension about your physical appearance and leads to the truth that "beauty glows from within."

Take it upon yourself to select a closing moment within your Incident that alleviates previous tension. Select an instant that leads to your truth, just as the compliment in the pimply prom story led to the truth about beauty. Keep in mind that the moment does not have to be larger than life; the best stories consists of subtle, simple instants that awaken our souls. Also, you might not find your resolution in the incident. Your resolution might come years later in another scenario related to the incident. That's okay. Sometimes, it requires years of learning for us to understand what the Spirit is saying to us. *(Read my parable called, "Loss" as an example of this delayed resolution.)*

6. Participants share about the wrong ways in which they sought for closure, or Resolution, relating to their painful past.

7. Participants share about the Resolution that God gave them pertaining to their Incident.

8. The Facilitator reviews the homework assignment for this week. The Facilitator encourages the Participants to share their homework assignments on the social media platform throughout the week, relating to this session.

*What did the Holy Spirit show you in this session?*

_____

_____

_____

_____

_____

_____

_____

_____

_____

_____

_____

_____

_____

_____

_____

_____

_____

_____

_____

_____

_____

_____

_____

# Homework Assignment Seven:  R – *Resolution*

"Now, we who have believed enter that rest" (Heb.4:3).

1. Elaborate upon the Resolution that God gave you relating to your Incident._____

_____

_____

_____

_____

_____

_____

_____

_____

_____

_____

_____

_____

_____

_____

_____

_____

_____

_____

_____

_____

_____

_____

_____

_____

_____

_____

_____

2. Elaborate upon how that Resolution has brought rest to your heart and mind._____

_____

_____

_____

_____

_____

_____

_____

_____

_____

_____

_____

_____

_____

_____

_____

_____

_____

_____

_____

_____

_____

_____

_____

_____

_____

_____

_____

# Session Eight: *E – Empathy*

1. Prayer for the help of the Holy Spirit.

2. Read the ground rules.

3. Participants introduce themselves by saying: "My name is.........and one lesson I've learned in my life is........."

4. Participant reads the following bible verse about Empathy: "Be kind and compassionate to one another, forgiving each other, just as in Christ God forgave you" (Eph. 4:32).

5. Participant reads the following section from the book on Empathy:
Empathy is defined as seeing with another person's eyes, thinking with another person's mind, and feeling with another person's heart. According to neuroscience, there resides eleven empathic circuits in the brain that enable us to empathize; sadly, some people's empathic circuits short-circuited at some point during life. Empathy allows you as the writer to take into account the perspectives of others within your story. This Empathy supplants all narrow, judgmental thinking. When you write, show Empathy towards your younger self, your opponents, your authorities and whoever else plays a role in your story. Empathizing with the characters of your story will add depth and dimension by showing multiple perspectives.

Also, the value of Empathy is that it helps you forgive the people who hurt you by understanding their handicaps. Chances are, it would be easy to pardon a blind person who knocked over a vase in your house because you understand their limitations. Likewise, the people who injured you are handicapped in some fashion; for instance, limited in the areas of love, respect or consideration. Empathizing with their handicaps, through your writing, makes forgiveness more bearable. This simply means shedding light on their own struggles, or giving them a voice, in your story. Keep in mind, Empathy does not *excuse* bad behavior, but *explains* it.

Lastly, it benefits you tremendously to empathize with God. When you catch His divine perspective, it keeps you from getting stuck in one isolated moment. Instead, His viewpoint enables you to behold a bigger picture. When you gaze at the earth's landscape from an airplane, you do not get overwhelmed by the graffiti on a sidewalk or the bad paint-job on a house; instead, a view of the big picture takes your breath away. Likewise, perceiving your past through divine lens allows you to see how God weaves all of your moments together into one beautiful tapestry.

This kind of empathy becomes obtainable when you pray (which opens your spirit), read the sacred scriptures (which opens your mind) and engage in relationship with other believers (which opens your heart). Incorporate this kind of empathy within your story by expounding upon the manner in which God weaved your pain into His purposes.

6. Participants empathize with their younger self in their selected Incident for two to three minutes.

7. Participants empathize with other characters in their selected Incident for two to three minutes.

8. Participants empathize with God's viewpoint in their selected Incident for two to three minutes.

9. Facilitator reviews the homework assignment for this week. Facilitator encourages the Participants to share their homework assignment on the social media platform throughout the week, relating to this session.

*What did the Holy Spirit show you in this session?*

_____

_____

_____

_____

_____

_____

_____

_____

_____

_____

_____

_____

_____

_____

_____

_____

_____

_____

_____

_____

_____

_____

_____

_____

_____

_____

_____

# Homework Assignment Eight: *E – Empathy*

"Be kind and compassionate to one another, forgiving each other, just as in Christ God forgave you" (Eph. 4:32).

1. Empathize with your younger self in your selected Incident.

_____

_____

_____

_____

_____

_____

_____

_____

_____

_____

_____

_____

_____

_____

_____

_____

2. Empathize with other characters in your selected Incident.

_____

_____

_____

_____

_____

_____

_____

_____

_____

_____

_____

_____

_____

_____

_____

_____

3. Empathize with God's viewpoint in your selected Incident.

_____

_____

_____

_____

_____

_____

_____

_____

_____

_____

_____

_____

_____

_____

_____

_____

_____

_____

# Session Nine:
## *The Parables*

1. Prayer for the help of the Holy Spirit.

2. Read the ground rules.

3. Participants introduce themselves by saying: "My name is.........and one lesson I've learned in my life is........."

4. Participants share their final parable.

5. Participants share feedback to one other about their parables. The feedback should correlate to the P.I.C.T.U.R.E. formula.

*"Pick up your mat, and walk." (John 5:8).*
Take a P.I.C.T.U.R.E. of _____

*P - Pain*

_____
_____
_____
_____
_____

*I - Incident*

_____
_____
_____
_____
_____

*C - Conflict*

_____
_____
_____
_____
_____

*T - Truth*

_____
_____
_____
_____
_____

*U – Unfolding Action*

_____

_____

_____

_____

_____

*R – Resolution*

_____

_____

_____

_____

_____

*E - Empathy*

_____

_____

_____

_____

_____

*A Parable about* _____

_____

_____

_____

_____

_____

_____

_____

*"Pick up your mat, and walk" (John 5:8).*
Take a P.I.C.T.U.R.E. of _____

*P - Pain*

_____
_____
_____
_____
_____

*I - Incident*

_____
_____
_____
_____
_____

*C - Conflict*

_____
_____
_____
_____
_____

*T - Truth*

_____
_____
_____
_____
_____

*U – Unfolding Action*

_____

_____

_____

_____

_____

*R – Resolution*

_____

_____

_____

_____

_____

*E - Empathy*

_____

_____

_____

_____

_____

*A Parable about* _____

_____

_____

_____

_____

_____

_____

_____

*"Pick up your mat, and walk" (John 5:8).*
Take a P.I.C.T.U.R.E. of _____

*P - Pain*

_____

_____

_____

_____

_____

*I - Incident*

_____

_____

_____

_____

_____

*C - Conflict*

_____

_____

_____

_____

_____

*T - Truth*

_____

_____

_____

_____

_____

*U – Unfolding Action*

_____

_____

_____

_____

_____

*R – Resolution*

_____

_____

_____

_____

_____

*E - Empathy*

_____

_____

_____

_____

_____

*A Parable about* _____

_____

_____

_____

_____

_____

_____

_____

*"Pick up your mat, and walk" (John 5:8).*
Take a P.I.C.T.U.R.E. of _____

*P - Pain*

_____
_____
_____
_____
_____

*I - Incident*

_____
_____
_____
_____
_____

*C - Conflict*

_____
_____
_____
_____
_____

*T - Truth*

_____
_____
_____
_____
_____

*U – Unfolding Action*

_____
_____
_____
_____
_____

*R – Resolution*

_____
_____
_____
_____
_____

*E - Empathy*

_____
_____
_____
_____
_____

*A Parable about* _____

_____
_____
_____
_____
_____
_____
_____
_____

*"Pick up your mat, and walk" (John 5:8).*
Take a P.I.C.T.U.R.E. of _____

*P - Pain*

_____

_____

_____

_____

_____

*I - Incident*

_____

_____

_____

_____

_____

*C - Conflict*

_____

_____

_____

_____

_____

*T - Truth*

_____

_____

_____

_____

_____

*U – Unfolding Action*

_____
_____
_____
_____
_____

*R – Resolution*

_____
_____
_____
_____
_____

*E - Empathy*

_____
_____
_____
_____
_____

*A Parable about* _____

_____
_____
_____
_____
_____
_____
_____
_____

*"Pick up your mat, and walk"* (John 5:8).

Take a P.I.C.T.U.R.E. of _____

*P - Pain*

_____

_____

_____

_____

_____

*I - Incident*

_____

_____

_____

_____

_____

*C - Conflict*

_____

_____

_____

_____

_____

*T - Truth*

_____

_____

_____

_____

_____

*U – Unfolding Action*

_____
_____
_____
_____
_____

*R – Resolution*

_____
_____
_____
_____
_____

*E - Empathy*

_____
_____
_____
_____
_____

*A Parable about* _____

_____
_____
_____
_____
_____
_____
_____

*"Pick up your mat, and walk" (John 5:8).*

Take a P.I.C.T.U.R.E. of _____

*P - Pain*

_____

_____

_____

_____

_____

*I - Incident*

_____

_____

_____

_____

_____

*C - Conflict*

_____

_____

_____

_____

_____

*T - Truth*

_____

_____

_____

_____

_____

*U – Unfolding Action*

_____

_____

_____

_____

_____


*R – Resolution*

_____

_____

_____

_____

_____


*E - Empathy*

_____

_____

_____

_____

_____


*A Parable about* _____

_____

_____

_____

_____

_____

_____

_____

*"Pick up your mat, and walk" (John 5:8).*
Take a P.I.C.T.U.R.E. of _____

*P - Pain*

_____

_____

_____

_____

_____

*I - Incident*

_____

_____

_____

_____

_____

*C - Conflict*

_____

_____

_____

_____

_____

*T - Truth*

_____

_____

_____

_____

_____

*U – Unfolding Action*

_____

_____

_____

_____

_____


*R – Resolution*

_____

_____

_____

_____

_____


*E - Empathy*

_____

_____

_____

_____

_____


*A Parable about* _____

_____

_____

_____

_____

_____

_____

_____

*"Pick up your mat, and walk." (John 5:8).*
Take a P.I.C.T.U.R.E. of _____

*P - Pain*

_____
_____
_____
_____
_____

*I - Incident*

_____
_____
_____
_____
_____

*C - Conflict*

_____
_____
_____
_____
_____

*T - Truth*

_____
_____
_____
_____
_____

*U – Unfolding Action*

_____
_____
_____
_____

*R – Resolution*

_____
_____
_____
_____

*E - Empathy*

_____
_____
_____
_____

*A Parable about* _____

_____
_____
_____
_____
_____
_____
_____

*"Pick up your mat, and walk." (John 5:8).*
Take a P.I.C.T.U.R.E. of _____

*P - Pain*

_____
_____
_____
_____
_____

*I - Incident*

_____
_____
_____
_____
_____

*C - Conflict*

_____
_____
_____
_____
_____

*T - Truth*

_____
_____
_____
_____
_____

*U – Unfolding Action*

_____

_____

_____

_____

_____


*R – Resolution*

_____

_____

_____

_____

_____


*E - Empathy*

_____

_____

_____

_____

_____


*A Parable about* _____

_____

_____

_____

_____

_____

_____

_____

*"Pick up your mat, and walk." (John 5:8).*
Take a P.I.C.T.U.R.E. of _____

*P - Pain*

_____
_____
_____
_____
_____

*I - Incident*

_____
_____
_____
_____

*C - Conflict*

_____
_____
_____
_____

*T - Truth*

_____
_____
_____
_____

*U – Unfolding Action*

_____
_____
_____
_____
_____

*R – Resolution*

_____
_____
_____
_____
_____

*E - Empathy*

_____
_____
_____
_____
_____

*A Parable about* _____

_____
_____
_____
_____
_____
_____
_____
_____

*"Pick up your mat, and walk" (John 5:8).*
Take a P.I.C.T.U.R.E. of _____

*P - Pain*

_____
_____
_____
_____
_____

*I - Incident*

_____
_____
_____
_____
_____

*C - Conflict*

_____
_____
_____
_____
_____

*T - Truth*

_____
_____
_____
_____
_____

*U – Unfolding Action*

_____

_____

_____

_____

_____


*R – Resolution*

_____

_____

_____

_____

_____


*E - Empathy*

_____

_____

_____

_____

_____


*A Parable about* _____

_____

_____

_____

_____

_____

_____

_____

*"Pick up your mat, and walk" (John 5:8).*

Take a P.I.C.T.U.R.E. of _____

*P - Pain*

_____

_____

_____

_____

_____

*I - Incident*

_____

_____

_____

_____

*C - Conflict*

_____

_____

_____

_____

*T - Truth*

_____

_____

_____

_____

*U – Unfolding Action*

_____

_____

_____

_____

_____

*R – Resolution*

_____

_____

_____

_____

_____

*E - Empathy*

_____

_____

_____

_____

_____

*A Parable about* _____

_____

_____

_____

_____

_____

_____

_____

*"Pick up your mat, and walk" (John 5:8).*
Take a P.I.C.T.U.R.E. of _____

*P - Pain*

_____

_____

_____

_____

_____

*I - Incident*

_____

_____

_____

_____

_____

*C - Conflict*

_____

_____

_____

_____

_____

*T - Truth*

_____

_____

_____

_____

_____

*U – Unfolding Action*

_____
_____
_____
_____
_____

*R – Resolution*

_____
_____
_____
_____
_____

*E - Empathy*

_____
_____
_____
_____
_____

*A Parable about* _____

_____
_____
_____
_____
_____
_____
_____

 *Acknowledgments*

To my Father in heaven, it was your mighty hand that plucked me out of the many pits along the way (even those pits I leaped into), it was your grace that sustained me, and it was your plan to predestine me for greatness.

To my parents, Michael and Dawn, despite your youthfulness, it was your continual efforts of love and commitment that instilled confidence within me.

To my children, Ashley, Mikie, Hannah and Olivia, it was your arrival on this planet that motivated me to be a better man.

To my Aunt Rose, it was your hospitality that kept me sane during one of the most trying times of my life, and throughout the writing of this book.

To my grandfather, Fred, it was the memory of sitting on your lap, striking the keys on your typewriter, that inspired me to be an author. You left me your mantle when you went home.

To Colleen Mellor, it was your tenacious investment in my tenth grade English class that caused me to win a state-wide award and take my writing skills seriously.

To Bishop Jeff Williams, it was your words: "Stop treating it like a hobby! Start treating it like an assignment!" that helped me get the job done.

To my older brother, Scott Axtmann, it was your discipleship that taught me how to pray, fast, read my bible and love people unconditionally.

To my spiritual father, Pasco Manzo, it was your leadership, mentorship and role-modelling that made a man out of me on every level of my life.

To my opponents, with all forgiveness, sincerity and love, I owe you a letter of gratitude for the opportunities you gave me to grow in Christ-likeness.

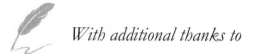 *With additional thanks to*

Rebecca Danielle of *Radiance by Rebecca Photography*
for the photographs of Michael.

Simone Spruce of *simonespruce.com*
for the title page illustration.

William Armitage of *Words in the Works*
for book design.

## *About the Author*

Michael A. Caparrelli, PhD (abd) served for sixteen years as a pastor of a recovery church in Rhode Island. Currently, he is in the final dissertation stage of his PhD in Behavioral Science, investigating the impact of church on the recovery journey of adults with addictions.

He travels across the nation, speaking to churches, schools, prisons and rehabs, on a variety of subjects in behavioral health from a faith-based perspective.

He has four children—Ashley, Mikie, Hannah and Olivia. He is a devout follower of Jesus Christ.

*If you would like to book Michael for a speaking engagement, please email him at: Michaelcaparrelli@unmuted.app*

Made in the USA
Middletown, DE
16 January 2020

82911168R10066